MW01538659

Table of Contents

Introduction

Let's be honest. While the Harry Potter series is known as a favourite for kids and tweens, it is just as popular with the adults as the youth. That is why this Harry Potter cocktail book is an essential for any party you throw for your fellow witches and wizards. If you are looking for some beverages to set the mood for your gathering, these cocktails are sure to inspire and delight your guests. When the occasion calls for something smoky and spooky, try the

Flaming Dragon's Blood cocktail of wrap your lips around the blood-sucking bat for an otherworldly taste.

Author's Note

Some of the recipes contain dry ice which is tricky to handle. Always use bowls and instruments that are safe to use with dry ice and always wear gloves to prevent burns. Dry ice crates very cool effects when you add hot water and handled with extreme care.

1. Happy Elf cocktail

Noblepig.com

House elves are industrious characters in the Harry Potter series. Dobby, the house elf, is the inspiration for this cocktail when he became a free elf.

Preparation Time-5 minutes
Servings – 1
Ingredients:

- 2 ounces Absolut Citron vodka
- 1 ounce Midori liqueur
- 1 ounce white cranberry juice
- Maraschino cherries

Directions:

Place the ice in a cocktail shaker and then add all of the **Ingredients**. Shake very well until combined. Strain the cocktail in to a glass and top with a maraschino

2. Flaming Dragon's Blood cocktail

Hagrid's beloved dragon Norbert is the inspiration for this amazing cocktail. I like to garnish this drink with a spear of raspberries or slice of pineapple.

Preparation Time-5 minutes
Servings – 1
Ingredient:

- Blood Syrup
- 12 ounces frozen raspberries
- 3 sprigs of thyme
- 4 ounces white sugar
- 4 ounces of water
- Brown food coloring
- Cocktail
- 2 fluid ounces Bacardi Superior
- 1½ ounces blood syrup
- ¾ ounce lemon juice

- 2 ice cubes
- ⅛ teaspoon of Wilton Red Luster Dust
- 1/3 ounce rum

Directions:

Blood Syrup

1. Heat raspberries, thyme, white sugar and water in a saucepan on medium high heat.

2. Bring mixture to a boil, stirring constantly until sugar dissolves and raspberries are soft.

3. Remove from the heat and cool to the room temperature. Run syrup through a fine mesh sieve and pour syrup into a sealable container. Place in refrigerator.

Cocktail

1. Combine Bacardi, blood syrup, lemon juice, ice cubes, red luster dust and rum in a cocktail shaker. Shake vigorously for about 5 seconds and strain into a cocktail glass.

2. Place spoon on the surface of glass and layer blood syrup on the surface.

3. Hair of Cerberus

I like to start with 3 ounces of gin and ¼ ounce of lemon juice when I want a drink that is lighter on the alcohol. Be very careful with the peppers, don't touch your eyes or lips after handling them unless you wash them thoroughly.

Preparation Time-5 minutes
Servings – 1
Ingredients:

- 1/2 ounce fresh lemon juice
- 3 dashes Tabasco
- 6 ounces Bulldog Gin
- 1 slice of chili pepper

Directions:

1. Combine gin and Tabasco in a cocktail shaker with ice and shake vigorously

2. Strain the mixture in to a cocktail glass and then top with chili pepper.

4. Mudblood cocktail

Popular belief was that Purebloods were the most powerful of witches and wizards. This theory was disproven by Hermione, who was a mudblood and possessed superior qualities.

Preparation Time-5 minutes
Servings - 1
Ingredients:

- 1 ½ ounces Vodka
- 1 ½ ounces Baileys Irish Cream
- 1 ½ ounces Coffee liqueur

Directions:

Mix all **Ingredients** in a martini shaker with ice and shake vigorously. Pour liquid into a martini glass and top with coffee beans.

5. Pureblood Cocktail

The Weasleys were of pureblood as both of their parents contained mystical powers. I dedicate this cocktail to Ron Weasley and his family who always made Harry feel welcome.

Preparation Time-5 minutes
Ingredients:

- 6 ounces licorice liqueur
- 4 ½ ounces blackcurrant cordial
- 12 ounces water
- black food coloring
- 8 ounces sugar

Directions:

1. Pour water into a pitcher filled with water and add food coloring until desired colour is reached. Stir vigorously after every drop of food coloring.

2. Fill ice cube tray with black water and freeze until solid.

3. Combine 8 ounces of white sugar and ¼ teaspoon of food coloring in a large bowl and mix until completely incorporated.

4. Coat the rims of the glasses with black sugar. Fill each glass with a couple of ice cubes.

5. Mix liqueur, blackcurrant cordial and water in a large pitcher and pour into the glasses.

6. Witches blood brew

The dry ice in this drink creates an amazing spooky atmosphere when activated by the liquid. Be extra cautious when handling dry ice as it can cause burns.

Preparation Time-5 minutes
Ingredients:

- 8 medium blackberries
- 2 ounces 100% agave silver tequila
- 1 ounce freshly squeezed lemon juice
- 1 teaspoon maple syrup
- 5 fresh sage leaves
- 1 dash orange bitters
- Blackberries
- Dry Ice

Directions:

1. Mix berries and sage in a shaker and muddle until fragrant and crumbled down.

2. Pour silver tequila, lemon juice, orange bitters and maple syrup in a cocktail shaker. Mix vigorously and pour over dry ice in a glass.

7. Potter Pumpkin Cocktail

Pumpkins play an important role in the Harry Potter series. Whether being used as decorations, an excellent hiding place or an ingredient for pasties and juice, pumpkins make a delicious cocktail.

Preparation Time-5 minutes
Ingredients:

Punch

- 25 ¾ ounce spiced rum
- 8 ounces orange juice
- 8 ounces lemon juice
- 8 ounces spiced syrup
- 4 ounces pumpkin puree
- 20 ounces sparkling water
- cinnamon sticks

Spiced syrup

- 4 ounces demerara sugar
- 4 ounces water
- 6 whole cloves
- 6 allspice berries
- 1 cinnamon stick, broken into small pieces
- 1 star anise pod
- 6 white peppercorns
- 1/2 cracked nutmeg
- dry ice
- Hollowed out pumpkin

Directions:
Spiced syrup

1. Place cloves, allspice, cinnamon, star anise, peppercorns and nutmeg in a small pan and shake

back and forth over medium heat to prevent them from burning.

2. Add water and sugar to the mixture as soon as the spices in the pan become fragrant and toasted. Keep stirring until the sugar dissolves completely.

3. Bring mixture to a simmer and reduce heat to low. Cook for 10 minutes more and remove from heat.

4. Strain syrup through a strainer and cool completely

Punch

1. Combine spiced syrup, rum, orange juice, lemon juice, pumpkin puree and cinnamon sticks in a punch bowl safe for dry-ice.

2. Place a larger metal bowl in the hollowed out pumpkin and add dry ice to the bottom.

3. Pour punch through a strainer again and place in a bowl smaller than the bowl with dry ice

4. Place the punch bowl in the metal bowl. Stir punch and pour into small bowl.

5. Add sparkling water to the punch and stir.

6. Pour hot water into the metal bowl with the dry ice to activate it.

8. Witches Brew Punch

Serve this delicious punch at your next Potter Bash and create a magical atmosphere. The green color and smoky appearance gives this drink a mystical aura when served.

Preparation Time-5 minutes
Servings - 32
Ingredients:

- 67.62 ounces chilled ginger ale
- 32 ounces chilled pineapple juice
- 2 ½ ounces freshly squeezed lemon juice
- 128 ounces lime sherbet
- 90 ounce block dry ice
- punch bowl that fit inside cauldron
- Large cauldron

Directions:

1. Wearing gloves, carefully break dry ice into pieces with a mallet. Place some dry ice in the cauldron and store the rest safely in a cooler. Pour hot water over the dry ice in the cauldron so it starts to smoke.

2. Place a bowl that is safe to use with dry ice on top of the dry ice in the cauldron. Mix ginger ale, pineapple juice and lemon juice in the bowl and mix well.

3. Add sherbet to the punch and stir gently until it starts to melt. Serve and enjoy!

9. Dark Lord cocktail

This drink might sound strong and foreboding, but it was designed by Voldemort after all. Serve this with some blackberries on a cocktail spear.

Preparation Time-5 minutes
Servings – 1
Ingredients:

- 1 ounce blackberry schnapps
- 1 ounce vodka
- 1/2 ounce cranberry juice

Directions:

Combine schnapps, vodka and cranberry juice in a drink shaker and shake vigorously. Strain mixture into a chilled glass.

10. Blood-sucking bat cocktail

This cocktail commemorates the bats released during the Final Quidditch Cup. The syringe injected with syrup creates an amazing image of blood.

Preparation Time-5 minutes
Servings - 4
Ingredients:

- 16 ounces frozen raspberries
- 2 ounces amaretto
- 2 ounces white sugar
- 4 ounces vodka
- 6 ounces club soda
- 2 ounces orange juice
- 4 plastic syringes

Directions:

1. Place raspberries in a blender and process until pureed.

2. Place puree into a fine mesh sieve and press down to separate the seeds from the pulp. Discard seeds.

3. Mix raspberry puree with white sugar in a small pan on medium high heat.

4. Stir mixture often while it cooks until it is dark and thick. This should take about 10 minutes.

5. Place mixture in the refrigerator until chilled.

6. Combine amaretto, vodka and ice in a cocktail shaker and shake vigorously for 30 seconds. Add orange juice and club soda and stir. Pour into chilled glasses.

7. Fill a syringe with raspberry syrup mixture from the pan and inject into the cocktail before serving.

11. Bloody Baron Caesar

The Bloody Baron was a student at Hogwarts during the time knows as the "Founders' Time". He was one of several ghosts that inhabited the school while Harry Potter attended.

Preparation Time-5 minutes
Servings - 1
Ingredients:
Seasoned Salt

- ½ ounce sea salt
- Zest from ½ lime
- 1 teaspoon cilantro, finely chopped
- 1/8 teaspoon crushed hot pepper flakes
- 1 lime wedge

Bloody Caesar

- 6 ounces Clamato juice
- 1 ounce vodka
- 1/3 ounce lime juice
- 1/4 teaspoon Tabasco sauce
- 1/4 teaspoon Worcestershire sauce
- 1 lime wedge
- 1 stalk celery
- 1 stalk cilantro
- Ice cubes

Directions:

1. To make the salt mixture, stir sea salt, lime zest, cilantro and pepper flakes in a bowl.

2. Circle the rim of the glass with the lime wedge to moisten and dip in the sea salt mixture.

Bloody Caesar

3. Mix Clamato, vodka, lime juice, Tabasco and Worcestershire in a bowl until well combined.

4. Fill glasses ¾ of the way with ice cubes and pour in the Bloody Caesar mixture.

5. Garnish with cilantro and celery and add a lime wedge to the rim

12. Nearly Headless Nick's Deathday cocktail

Nearly Headless Nick was another ghost at Hogwarts who celebrated his death day with a big party. This cocktail would be the best way to celebrate the anniversary of Nearly Headless Nick's death at your Potterfest.

Preparation Time-5 minutes
Servings - 1
Ingredients:

- 1 ounce vodka
- 1 ounce cream
- 1 ounce dark cacao liqueur
- 1 ounce Triple Sec
- 1 orange

Directions:

Combine vodka, cream, cacao liqueur, Triple sec and ice in a cocktail shaker. Vigorously shake and strain into a cocktail glass. Decorate with orange slices.

13. Liquid Luck Cocktail

There are many variations of this lucky golden cocktail dedicated to the Golden Snitch. I have served this with some pearl onions on a cocktail spear to make it extra festive.

Preparation Time-5 minutes
Ingredients:

- ¼ teaspoon gold shimmery luster dust
- 5 ½ ounces St-Germain liqueur
- 2 ½ ounces vodka

Directions:

Mix all the **Ingredients** in a cocktail shaker and then vigorously shake. Strain into a cocktail glass and chill.

14. GOLD SHIMMERY BUBBLY MOCKTAIL

When you want to celebrate Harry Potter without alcohol, this mocktail will look and taste festive without the hangover. Garnish this drink with some raspberries or blackberries for a decorative look.

Preparation Time-5 minutes
Ingredients:

- ¼ teaspoon gold shimmery luster dust
- 5 ½ ounces St-Germain liqueur
- 2 ½ ounces vodka
- Chilled sparkling white grape juice

Directions:

1. Make Liquid Luck cocktails and pour ¾ of an ounce into champagne flutes.

2. Pour 4 ounces of sparkling grape juice into each champagne flute and serve

15. Golden snitch golden champagne cocktail

This cocktail is the third golden cocktail named after the golden snitch in Quidditch. I like to use Prosecco but any champagne or sparkling wine will work.

Preparation Time-5 minutes
Servings - 1
Ingredients:

- ¼ teaspoon gold shimmery luster dust
- 2 ½ ounces elderflower cordial
- 2 ½ ounces vodka
- 25 ¾ ounces Prosecco

Directions:

GOLD SHIMMERY CHAMPAGNE COCKTAIL

1. Make Liquid Luck cocktails and pour ¾ of an ounce into champagne flutes.

2. Pour 4 ounces of Prosecco into each champagne flute and serve

16. The Grey Lady

The Grey Lady was another ghost from Harry Potter who inhabited Ravenclaw House. Her real name was Helena Ravenclaw and she was the object of desire for another ghost, The Bloody Baron.

Preparation Time-5 minutes
Servings - 1
Ingredients:

- 1 ¾ ounce Grey Goose L'Orange Flavored Vodka
- 1 ½ ounces fresh lemon juice
- 1 ¼ ounce simple syrup
- 1 ¼ ounce Creme de Violette
- 1 dash peach bitters

Directions:

Combine vodka, lemon juice, simple syrup, Crème de violette and peach bitters in a cocktail shaker with ice. Strain in to a martini glass and serve.

17. Fluffy's Dark cocktail

Fluffy was the ironic name for the three-headed dog belonging to Hagrid. The animal helped Hogwarts by protecting The Philosopher's Stone. The monstrous animal had one weakness, he would fall asleep at the sound of music.

Preparation Time – 3 minutes
Servings – 1
Ingredients:

- 2 ounces Smirnoff Marshmallow vodka
- 2 ounces Godiva Dark Chocolate liqueur
- 1 ounce cream
- 4 mini marshmallows
- Sweetened cocoa powder

Directions:
1. Combine vodka, liqueur and cream in a cocktail shaker with ice and shake vigorously.

2. Strain into a chilled glass and top with marshmallows. Sprinkle with cocoa powder.

18. Dragon's heart cocktail

This cocktail is another recipe named for the dragon Hagrid had as a pet for a short time. Garnish with blood orange slices or slices of pink grapefruit.

Preparation Time- 5 minutes
Servings – 1
Ingredients:

- 3 wedges of lime
- 3/4 ounces elderflower cordial

- 5 drops of Angostura Bitters
- 1 1/2 ounces rum
- 1/2 ounces ginger liqueur
- 3/4 ounces mezcal
- 1 1/2 ounces blood orange juice
- blood orange slice

Directions:

1. Muddle lime, cordial and 3 drops of Angostura bitters together. Add rum, liqueur, mezcal and orange juice in a shaker with ice and shake well.

2. Strain in to a martini glass and top with bitters and slices of blood orange

19. Wizard's brew

This brew is the perfect drink to serve when your fellow wizards and witches are over for a get-together. I like to add dry ice to the glasses to create a smoky effect.

Preparation Time- 10 minutes
Servings – 4
Ingredients:

- 8 ounces light brown sugar
- 1 ounce water
- 3 ounce butter
- 1/2 teaspoon salt
- 1/2 teaspoon apple cider vinegar
- 6 ounces heavy cream, divided
- 1/2 teaspoon rum extract
- 48 ounces cream soda

Directions:

1. Mix the sugar and water in a small pan and bring to a gentle boil. Cook until a candy thermometer reads 240 degrees Fahrenheit.

2. Stir in salt, butter, ¼ cream and vinegar until combined. Remove from the heat and cool to the room temperature.

3. Stir rum extract into the mixture once it has cooled.

4. Beat 1 ounce of the sugar mixture and the rest of the cream in a bowl with an electric mixer for 2 - 3 minutes until thickened.

5. Evenly divide brown sugar mixture from the pan into 4 glasses and add 2 ounces of cream soda to each glass. Stir and fill each glass to the top with whipped cream.

20. Goblet of fire

If you have a Smoking Cloche (Fortessa) and place the glass inside, it will create an amazing effect. Turn off the cloche so that cocktail fills with smoke for a few minutes.

Preparation Time- 5 minutes
Servings - 1
Ingredients:

- 2 ounces of whiskey
- 2 dashes of bitters
- 1 orange peel
- 2 sugar cubes
- 1 rosemary sprig

Directions:

1. Run the orange peel around the rim of a whiskey glass

2. Fill glass with whiskey, bitters and sugar cubes. Stir until sugar dissolves

3. Top drink with rosemary

21. Polyjuice

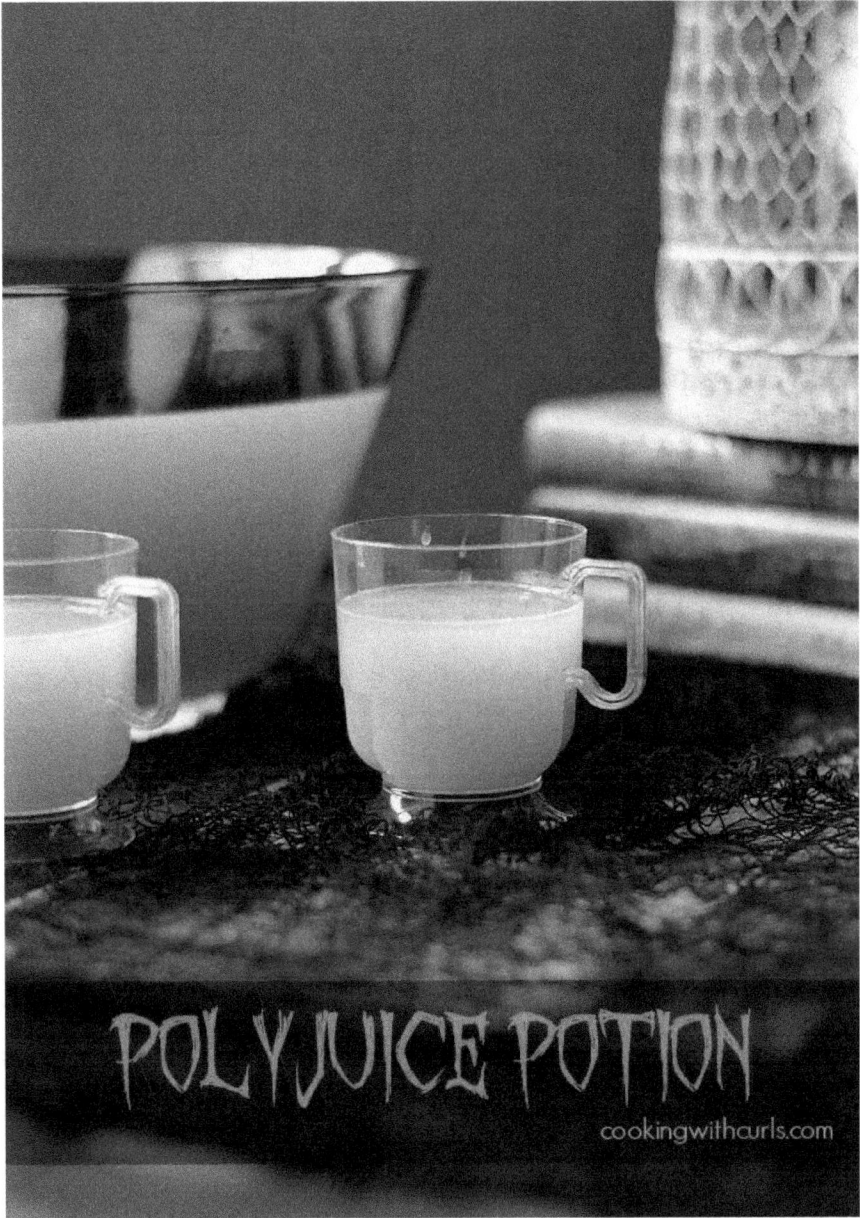

POLYJUICE POTION

cookingwithcurls.com

This polyjuice potion may not let you assume the appearance of someone else, but it will set the tone for your Harry Potter book club. I like to add some dry ice to this to create a more 'potion-like' appearance.

Preparation Time – 5 minutes
Servings – 1
Ingredients:

- 2 ounces of pomegranate juice
- ½ juiced lime
- 2 ounces of tequila
- Ginger Ale

Directions:

1. Combine pomegranate juice, lime juice and tequila in a large glass and stir for 20 seconds.

2. Fill with ginger ale ¾ of the way up. Add a piece of dry ice the size of an ice cube and serve.

22. Elderflower Wand Apple Martini

This martini will taste delicious with some Potter-inspired nibbles at your next party. I like to add some minimarshmallows in the drink for extra sweetness.

Preparation Time-5 minutes
Servings – 1
Ingredients:

- 1 Ounce of Elderflower Liqueur
- 1 Ounce of vodka
- 1 Ounce of apple juice
- 1 Tablespoon of honey
- Juice of half a lime
- Ice
- Green Apple Slices

Directions:

1. Combine all **Ingredients** except for apple slices in a cocktail shaker and shake vigorously for 20 seconds.

2. Strain in to a martini glass and top off with 1 cube of dry ice and apple slices

23. Voldemort cocktail

Voldemort's cocktail is spicy, dark and delicious. This cocktail is served with black ice cubes and a slice of jalapeno.

Preparation Time- 10 minutes
Servings – 4
Ingredients:

- 1 ounce tequila
- 1 ounce tabasco sauce
- 1 jalapeno pepper, thinly sliced

Directions:

Muddle Tequila and Tabasco and strain into a shot glass. Top with pepper slices

24. Bellatrix Lestrange

Bellatrix is one of Voldemort's most loyal followers in the Potter series. She was a Death Eater when she graduated from Hogwarts.

Ingredients:

- 1 ounce Absolut Vodka
- 1 ounce Bailey's Irish cream
- 1 ounce Amaretto
- 1 ounce heavy cream
- Chocolate syrup
- Ground cinnamon
- Crushed almonds

Directions:

1. Chill a martini glass in the freezer.

2. Combine vodka, Bailey's, Amaretto and cream in a cocktail shaker and shake vigorously for 20-30 seconds.

3. Place chocolate syrup around the inside of the rim of the martini glass

4. Pour liquid into the glass and top with cinnamon and almonds

25. Fleur Delacour cocktail

Fleur married the eldest son of the Weasley's pureblood family and brother to Ron Weasley. She was a loyal and talented wife and mother.

Ingredients:

- 3 ounces Nuvo Sparkling Liqueur
- 1 ounce Absolut Vodka
- 1 Strawberry
- 3 Raspberries

Directions:

1. Combine the vodka and ice in a cocktail shaker and then shake vigorously for 20 seconds

2. Arrange raspberries in the bottom of a champagne flute

3. Pour chilled vodka over the raspberries and add Nuvo Top with a strawberry on a cocktail spear

26. Fred and George Weasley twin cocktail

These brothers are better known as the Weasley twins in the Harry Potter books. Serve this cocktail in twos to your guests when you throw your big bash.

Ingredients:

- 1 ounce Absolut Vodka
- ½ ounce Chambord
- ½ ounce Peach Schnapps
- 1 Splash of Pineapple juice
- Strawberry Pop Rocks

Directions:

1. Pour cold water into a martini glass and place in the freezer for 2-3 minutes.

2. Combine vodka, Chambord, schnapps and pineapple juice in a cocktail shaker and shake vigorously for 20 seconds.

3. Coat the rim of the martini glass with candy and pour in liquid from the shaker.

27. Luna Lovegood

Luna Lovegood was part of House Ravenclaw and was the dreamy antithesis of Hermione Granger. This drink is the perfect match for Lovegood as it is sweet, sunny and a delicious mess of ideas.

Ingredients:

- 1 ounce Grey Goose Le Citron vodka
- ½ ounce Elderflower liquor
- 7 fresh raspberries
- 1 teaspoon white sugar
- Pink lemonade
- 1 lemon, cut in wedges

Directions:

1. Muddle raspberries and white sugar together in a tall glass.

2. Add ice cubes, vodka and lemonade. Garnish with lemon and 1 raspberry.

28. Minerva McGonagall

This cocktail is much like Professor McGonagall herself. It is tasteful, elegant without sweetness of any kind.

Ingredients:

- 2 ounces Absolut Vodka
- 6 ounce Earl Grey tea
- 1 dash simple syrup
- 1 ounce lemon juice
- 1 lemon, sliced
- 2 mint leaves

Directions:

1. Mix all **Ingredients** except for sliced lemon and mint leaves in a tall glass with ice and stir well.

2. Top with mint leaves and lemon slices

29. Slytherin cocktail

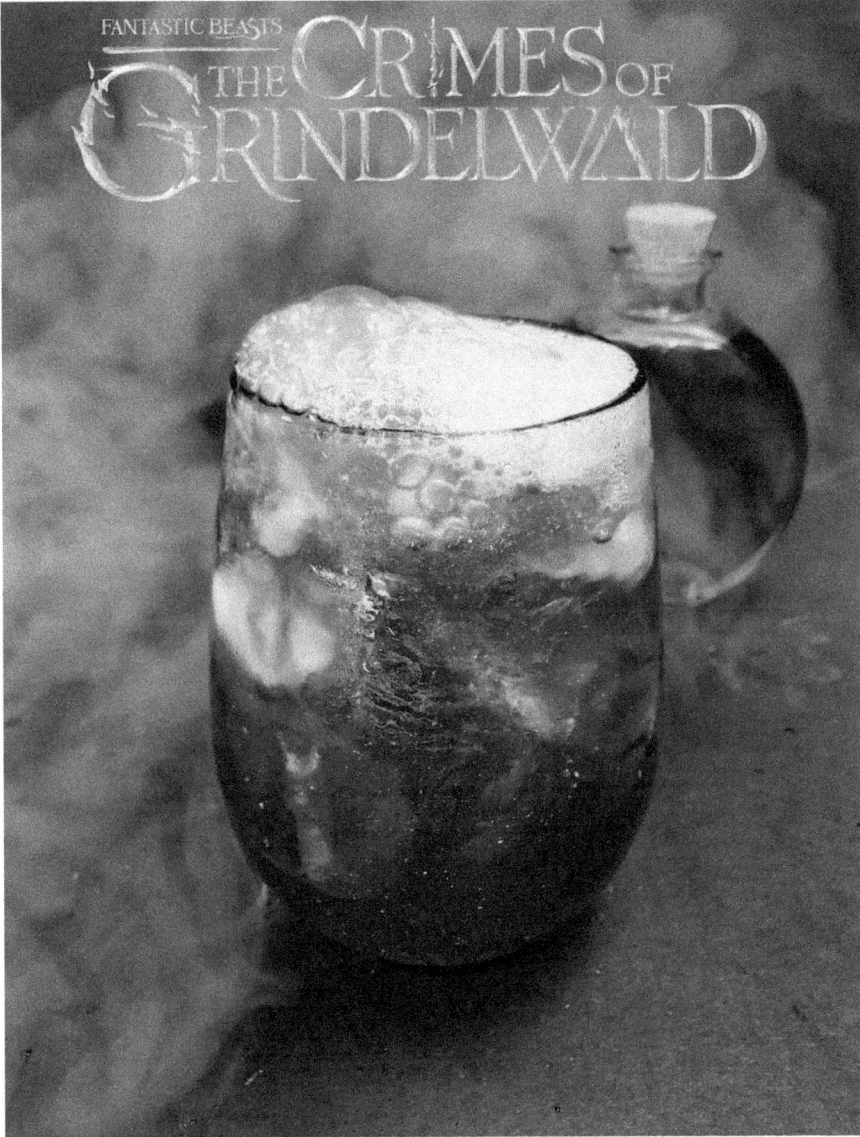

The Slytherin cocktail will liven up conversation at your next gathering. This sparkling cocktail is sparkly, tangy with a hint of a bite.

Ingredients:

- 1 ounce Bacardi rum
- 4 mint leaves
- 2 lime, slices
- 3 teaspoon white sugar
- 3 ounces Prosecco

Directions:

1. In a cocktail shaker, muddle mint, lime slices, rum and white sugar until sugar is dissolved.

2. Strain mixture into a champagne glass and pour in Prosecco. Top with mint leaves.

30. Black magic cocktail

Hogwarts teaches Black magic arts with great care at Hogwarts. This cocktail is a complex and magical concoction that sets the perfect tone for your Wizards' Party.

Ingredients:

- 1 ounce Aperol
- ½ ounce balsamic reduction

- 1 ounce freshly squeezed lime juice
- 1 ounce honey infused with rosemary, thyme and

oregano
- 1 ounce Grappa
- 4 fresh raspberries

Directions:

1. Add all the **Ingredients** in a shaker with the ice and shake vigorously for 20 seconds.

2. Strain in a glass filled with ice.

Conclusion

When you are looking for some inspired cocktails to serve at your Wizard's Bash, give one of these simple recipes a try. Harry Potter fans come in all different shapes, sizes and ages and celebrating the life and times of everyone's favourite Hogwarts student is cause for a drink! Serve one of these delicious cocktails and raise a glass of cheer to Harry Potter.

CPSIA information can be obtained
at www.ICGtesting.com
Printed in the USA
LVHW050102191120
672055LV00007B/119

9 781801 210058